SECURITY DOGS

by Bendix Anderson

Consultant: Wilma Melville, Founder
National Disaster Search Dog Foundation

New York, New York

Special thanks to Wilma Melville who founded the:
National Disaster Search Dog Foundation
206 N. Signal Street, Suite R
Ojai, CA 93023
(888) 4K9-HERO
www.SearchDogFoundation.org

The Search Dog Foundation is a not-for-profit organization that rescues dogs, gives them professional training, and partners them with firefighters to find people buried alive in disasters. They produce the most highly trained search dogs in the nation.

Special thanks to Barbara and Glen Simpson,
the owners of Rolling Meadow Kennel and Canine Training in Denton, North Carolina.
Thanks also to Officer Cathy Viverito and her canine partner, Pal,
of the New York City Police Department.

Design and production by Dawn Beard Creative and Octavo Design and Production, Inc.

Credits

Cover, Front (left), Shaun Best, Reuters / Corbis, (top right), AP / Wide World Photos; (center right), Ken Hammond / USDA Photo Library, (bottom right), AP / Wide World Photos; Back (top), AP / Wide World Photos, (center), Ken Hammond / USDA Photo Library, (bottom), AP / Wide World Photos. Title page, Shaun Best, Reuters / Corbis. Page 3, Dennis Light / Light Photographic; 4-5, AP / Wide World Photos; 6, AP / Wide World Photos; 6-7, Gerald L. Nino / US Customs & Border Protection, Department of Homeland Security; 8-9, Burstein Collection / CORBIS; 9, Library of Congress Prints & Photographs Collection; 10-11, Ken Hammond / USDA Photo Library; 11, Henry Ausloos / Animals Animals Earth Scenes; 12, AP / Wide World Photos; 13, Bill Turnbull / New York Daily News; 14-15, TNT Magazine / Alamy; 15, Fotosearch; 16, AP / Wide World Photos; 16-17, Tom Nebbia / CORBIS; 18-19, CORBIS; 19, Reuters / CORBIS; 20, 21, Dennis Light / Light Photographic; 22-23, Dale C. Sparta / CORBIS; 24-25, AP / Wide World Photos; 25, Ira Wyman / CORBIS SYGMA; 26-27, Tom Stewart / CORBIS; 27, Ken Hammond / USDA Photo Library; 28, Douglas Kirkland / CORBIS; 29(top left), Photodisc / Fotosearch; 29(top right), Photospin.com; 29(center), Tim Davis / Photo Researchers, Inc.; 29(bottom left), Yann Arthus-Bertrand / CORBIS; 29(bottom right), Photodisc / Fotosearch; 30, Tom Nebbia / Corbis.

Library of Congress Cataloging-in-Publication Data

Anderson, Bendix.
  Security dogs / by Bendix Anderson; consultant, Wilma Melville.
    p. cm.— (Dog heroes)
  Includes bibliographical references (p.   ).
  ISBN 1-59716-015-6 (lib. bdg) — ISBN 1-59716-038-5
  1. Police dogs—Juvenile literature. I. Melville, Wilma. II. Title. III. Series.

  HV8025.A53 2005
  363.2'32—dc22

                    2004021059

For more information, write to Bearport Publishing Company, Inc., 101 Fifth Avenue, Suite 6R, New York, New York 10003. Printed in the United States of America.

3 4 5 6 7 8 9 10

Table of Contents

Smells Like Trouble   4

A Strong Nose   6

The First Security Dogs   8

The Best Breeds   10

Big Dogs   12

A Dog Is Born   14

Security Dog School   16

Learning to Sniff   18

Training to Fight   20

On the Job   22

A Dangerous Job   24

The Future of Security Dogs   26

Just the Facts   28

Common Breeds:
   Security Dogs   29

Glossary   30

Bibliography   31

Read More   31

Learn More Online   31

Index   32

About the Author   32

Smells Like Trouble

Hundreds of bags and packages traveled through the airport that day. All of them had to be checked to make sure they didn't hide bombs, drugs, or other dangers.

Suddenly, the guard saw something on her X-ray screen. She couldn't tell exactly what it was, but it looked strange. She called over an officer and his security dog. Soon, the dog began to scratch at the suitcase. When the officer opened it, he found drugs hidden inside.

A security dog and his handler check a bag for dangerous items.

A security dog at a post office can check 400 to 500 packages in 30 minutes.

A Strong Nose

Security dogs search for things that are against the law. In airports, these animals smell suitcases to see if drugs are hidden inside. They sniff for guns at parades. They smell boxes to see if they hold bombs or other dangers.

At Kennedy Space Center, a security guard and his dog, Blesk, check equipment before it gets loaded onto the space shuttle.

At airports, dogs search for food in passengers' suitcases. Food from other countries might carry harmful bugs. These bugs could hurt our food crops.

Their good noses make well-trained security dogs better than people at finding things. Due to their size and four legs, they are also able to move through crowds more quickly and easily than people.

Dogs are trained to help officers at U.S. borders. This German shepherd is learning to find packages with dangerous things inside.

The First Security Dogs

Dogs and people have worked together for thousands of years. The first security dogs guarded people's homes. Back then, dogs didn't need to search for harmful things. They just needed to be faithful and strong. Today, people still use guard dogs to watch their homes and stores.

Native Americans used dogs to help them hunt for buffalo.

The police department in New York City began using dogs about 100 years ago. Soon, many police departments around the country had them on the **force**. About 40 years ago, people began training dogs to smell for bombs and drugs. Today, security dogs are **common** throughout the United States.

White House police dog King Tut and Officer W.S. Newton in 1929

About 9,000 security dogs work in the United States.

9

The Best Breeds

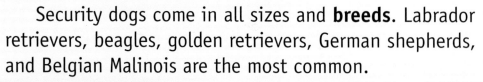

Security dogs come in all sizes and **breeds.** Labrador retrievers, beagles, golden retrievers, German shepherds, and Belgian Malinois are the most common.

Each dog's size decides the kind of work he will do. Beagles, for example, are the best dogs for searching people at airports. They are small and friendly. They don't frighten people. Beagles are also the right size for climbing among suitcases.

A beagle

Most beagles are only about 13 inches tall.

Comet, a member of the Beagle Brigade, at work at Dulles Airport in Washington, D.C.

11

Big Dogs

Most security dogs are a lot bigger than beagles. Labrador retrievers are almost a foot taller. They are good for sniffing large packages piled up at the post office. German shepherds and Belgian Malinois are even taller. Just the sight of them can scare some people.

The jaws of a German shepherd are strong enough to break someone's arm.

An airport guard and a German shepherd security dog patrol an airport in Moscow, the capital of Russia.

Big security dogs can be trained to catch people who do things against the law. A dog that works around crowds might find a person with a gun. If that person tries to run away, the dog can bite his arm. The dog won't let go until his **partner** comes to help.

A Dog Is Born

Some security dogs come from animal **shelters**. Others come from families who think their pets have the right skills for security work. The bigger animals usually come from dog **breeders** around the United States.

Most German shepherds that become security dogs are born in Europe. These dogs are very fit. They are also less likely to have health problems than dogs born in the United States.

German shepherd puppies

Many German shepherds work for the New York City Police Department. These dogs come from the Czech Republic, a country in Europe.

An animal shelter in England

Security Dog School

Dog breeders who raise animals for security work teach their puppies to follow **commands**. The puppies also begin to learn how to smell for hidden things. The animals best at finding things are sent to security dog school. Training begins when the dogs are two to three years old.

Apollo with his partner, Officer Stebbins, climbing up an eight-foot wall

Police Officer Greg Nester trains a German shepherd.

At school, dogs learn to climb around metal barrels. They learn to walk up ladders and down narrow boards. They also practice moving through tight places. On the job, they may need to squeeze inside a car trunk or slip through a hole in a fence.

Dogs spend from four to ten weeks at security dog school. The time spent depends on how much the dog knows when he begins.

Learning to Sniff

Dogs also learn special sniffing skills. These skills help them find certain drugs. The **trainer** brings the dog into a room filled with wooden boxes. One of the boxes holds the dog's favorite toy. The dog finds the toy quickly.

The toy is then hidden in the same box with a drug. The dog learns to find the toy by following the smell of the drug. Soon, the trainer hides just a little bit of the drug without the toy. When the dog finds it, the trainer gives him the toy as a reward.

A security dog practices sniffing for a bomb.

Security dogs also learn how to sniff for different powders that are used to make bombs.

Arro, a security dog, sniffs boxes looking for drugs.

Training to Fight

Some security dogs also learn how to fight. The trainer puts a heavy guard, called a sleeve, over his or her arm. The dog is trained to bite the sleeve. The animal learns that he should never bite unless the trainer tells him to attack.

For the last two weeks of training, the dog's new partner comes to school. The human and animal are taught how to work together and understand each other. The dog also learns to take orders only from his partner.

Dogs and handlers at a training school

Some dogs that are born in other countries never learn to follow commands in English. They only understand commands in the first language they learned.

On the Job

The airport can be a puzzling place for a dog on his first day of work. Each suitcase smells like a different person. When his partner gives the command to search for a smell, however, the dog knows what to do. He runs to the piles of suitcases and gets right to work.

Often a security dog can go a whole day without finding bombs or drugs. His partner, however, wants to keep the dog excited about searching. So he or she sometimes hides something for the animal to find.

Officer Paul Burkardt checks bags with his drug-sniffing dog on an airport runway.

A security dog usually spends his whole life with one partner.

A Dangerous Job

A person can become angry when a security dog finds drugs in his or her bag. He or she might attack the dog's partner or try to run away. No matter what happens, the security dog stays calm.

Being a security dog can be scary. What if someone has hidden a bomb? It could go off if it's touched. That's why security dogs are taught not to put their noses in people's bags. Instead, when the dog smells a bomb, he stands by the bag it is in or lays his nose against it.

Security dog and partner at Boston's Logan Airport

Security dogs are trained to ignore loud noises. They sit still even if a pot is dropped next to them.

Renza is checking this bag for bombs at the Tampa, Florida airport.

The Future of Security Dogs

Security dogs can work for five to eight years. By the time a dog is ten years old, he's ready to stop working. Many security dogs keep on living with their partners even when they are not on the job anymore.

Scientists are trying to build machines that are better than security dogs at finding things. They haven't been able to yet. It will be hard to make a machine that is smarter or braver than these amazing animals.

Dogs that search cars entering the United States work really hard. Many retire after only one to three years.

Just the Facts

- A dog's nose is naturally wet. He needs a wet nose in order to use his powerful sense of smell.

- Security dogs trained to search for food learn more than 100 different smells. They can sniff out apples, pears, meat, and many other foods.

- At U.S. airports, security dogs check the suitcases of over 40,000 flights every year.

- Some security dogs are trained to use **scent** to look for stolen money.

- A dog with lots of training can find a bomb 20 times faster than a person.

golden retriever

Labrador retriever

beagle

Belgian Malinois

German shepherd

breeders (BREE-durz) people who raise puppies

breeds (BREEDZ) types of a certain animal

commands (kuh-MANDZ) instructions given to be obeyed; orders

common (KOM-uhn) happening often or in large numbers

force (FORSS) a team of people who work together

partner (PART-nur) one of two or more people who do something
together

retire (ri-TIRE) to stop working; usually because of age

scent (SENT) the smell of an animal or person

security (si-KYOOR-i-tee) related to making something safe and free
from danger

shelters (SHEL-turz) places where animals that are not wanted
can stay

trainer (TRAYN-ur) someone who teaches a person or animal how to
do something

Bibliography

American Kennel Club. *The Complete Dog Book.* New York, NY: Howell Book House (1979).

Mesloh, Charles. *An Examination of Police Canine Use of Force in the State of Florida.* Orlando, FL: Department of Public Affairs in the College of Health and Public Affairs at the University of Central Florida (2003).

Silverstein, Alvin, and Virginia Silverstein. *Dogs: All About Them.* New York, NY: William Morrow (1986).

Singer, Marilyn. *A Dog's Gotta Do What a Dog's Gotta Do: Dogs at Work.* New York, NY: Henry Holt and Company (2000).

Read More

Bare, Colleen Stanley. *Sammy: Dog Detective.* New York, NY: Cobblehill Books/Dutton (1998).

Jackson, Donna. *Hero Dogs: Courageous Canines in Action.* New York, NY: Megan Tingley Books/Little, Brown and Company (2003).

Learn More Online

Visit these Web sites to learn more about security dogs:

www.dogswithjobs.com/about_dogs/about.htm

www.fbi.gov/kids/dogs/doghome.htm

Index

airports 4, 6, 11, 12, 22–23, 25, 28
animal shelters 14–15

beagles 10–11, 12, 29
Belgian Malinois 10, 12, 29
bombs 4, 6, 9, 19, 23, 25, 28
breeders 14, 16
breeds 10, 29

commands 16, 21, 22
Czech Republic 15

drugs 4–5, 6, 9, 18–19, 23, 24

Europe 15

fighting 20
food 6, 28

German shepherds 7, 10, 12, 15, 16, 29
golden retrievers 10, 29
guns 6, 13

homes 8
Labrador retrievers 10, 12, 29

Native Americans 8
New York City 9, 15

police department 9, 15
post office 5, 12
puppies 16

school 16–17, 21
scientists 27
smell 4, 6, 9, 16, 19, 22, 25, 28
sniffing 6, 12, 18–19, 23, 28

trainer 18–19, 20
training 9, 16–17, 20–21, 28

United States (U.S.) 9, 14–15, 27, 28

About the Author

Bendix Anderson has taught very young children at a therapeutic nursery and has worked in children's publishing. Today, when he's not writing children's books, he is a journalist writing about housing policy. He lives in Brooklyn, New York.